AF228547

INSIDE THE NBA

abdobooks.com

Published by Abdo Publishing, a division of ABDO, PO Box 398166, Minneapolis, Minnesota 55439. Copyright © 2023 by Abdo Consulting Group, Inc. International copyrights reserved in all countries. No part of this book may be reproduced in any form without written permission from the publisher. SportsZone™ is a trademark and logo of Abdo Publishing.

Printed in China.
052022
092022

Cover Photo: Matthew Stockman/Getty Images Sport/Getty Images
Interior Photos: Melinda Nagy/Shutterstock Images, 1; Mike Ehrmann/Getty Images Sport/Getty Images, 4; Mark J. Terrill/AP Images, 7, 8, 10; Douglas P. DeFelice/Getty Images Sport/Getty Images, 13; AP Images, 14; Lennox McLendon/AP Images, 16; Focus On Sport/Getty Images Sport/Getty Images, 18, 27; Gary Stewart/AP Images, 20, 29, 38; Darron Cummings/AP Images, 21; John Leyba/AP Images, 23; Focus On Sport/Getty Images, 24; David Zalubowski/AP Images, 30; Gerald Herbert/AP Images, 33; Focus On Sport/Getty Images Sport Classic/Getty Images, 34; Rick Stewart/Allsport/Hulton Archive/Getty Images, 36; Matt Slocum/AP Images, 40; Ronald Cortes/Getty Images Sport/Getty Images, 41

Editor: Charlie Beattie
Series Designer: Joshua Olson

Library of Congress Control Number: 2021951678

Publisher's Cataloging-in-Publication Data

Names: Graves, Will, author.
Title: Denver Nuggets / by Will Graves
Description: Minneapolis, Minnesota: Abdo Publishing, 2023 | Series: Inside the NBA | Includes online resources and index.
Identifiers: ISBN 9781532198250 (lib. bdg.) | ISBN 9781098271909 (ebook)
Subjects: LCSH: Denver Nuggets (Basketball team)--Juvenile literature. | Basketball--Juvenile literature. | Professional sports--Juvenile literature. | Sports franchises--Juvenile literature.
Classification: DDC 796.32364--dc23

TABLE OF
CONTENTS

CHAPTER ONE

NUGGETS CLIP THE CLIPPERS

The 2020 National Basketball Association (NBA) playoffs were unusual. The COVID-19 pandemic had forced the league to halt its season in March. For several months, people had to keep their distance from one another to slow the spread of the disease. Resuming the season, with teams traveling from city to city, would be too risky. Instead, the NBA returned that summer with a new plan. All of the playoff teams would meet near Orlando, Florida. There they were separated from the public. The setup became known as the NBA's "bubble."

The Denver Nuggets were one of the teams that traded their home arena for the bubble. They no longer had the comforts of playing at home, nor the support from fans. The longer a team lasted in the bubble, the longer its players would be away from their families. It would take toughness and mental strength to succeed there.

Denver's Nikola Jokić averaged 24.4 points, 9.8 rebounds, and 5.7 assists during the 2020 NBA playoffs.

The Nuggets clinched the third seed in the Western Conference. After getting past the Utah Jazz in seven games, they met a tough Los Angeles Clippers team. And after four games, the Clippers led the series 3–1. One more loss and Denver would be sent home. But Denver had been down this road before in these playoffs. The Nuggets knew they had what it took.

COMEBACK, PART ONE

The Nuggets had mostly been playoff pushovers in their NBA history—if they made the playoffs at all. The team, which joined the NBA in 1976, had never been to the Finals. Entering the 2020 playoffs, Denver had been to the postseason 11 times in the previous 24 seasons. In all but two of those appearances, the Nuggets failed to get out of the first round.

The 2020 Nuggets were ready to change that dismal history. The team had stars like high-scoring guard Jamal Murray. They also had 6-foot-11-inch center Nikola Jokić. The Serbian had finished ninth in NBA Most Valuable Player (MVP) voting. In just his fifth year in the league,

Jamal Murray, *center*, averaged 31.6 points per game during the Nuggets' 2020 playoff series victory over the Utah Jazz.

Jokić was already making a case for being one of the best players in Nuggets history.

Murray and Jokić had already led one comeback during the 2020 playoffs, against the Jazz. Denver had also trailed 3–1 in that series. Murray's 42 points helped the Nuggets avoid elimination in Game 5. Then the guard scored 50 to even the series in Game 6. Jokić took over in Game 7. He had 30 points and 14 rebounds as the Nuggets edged Utah 80–78 to win the series.

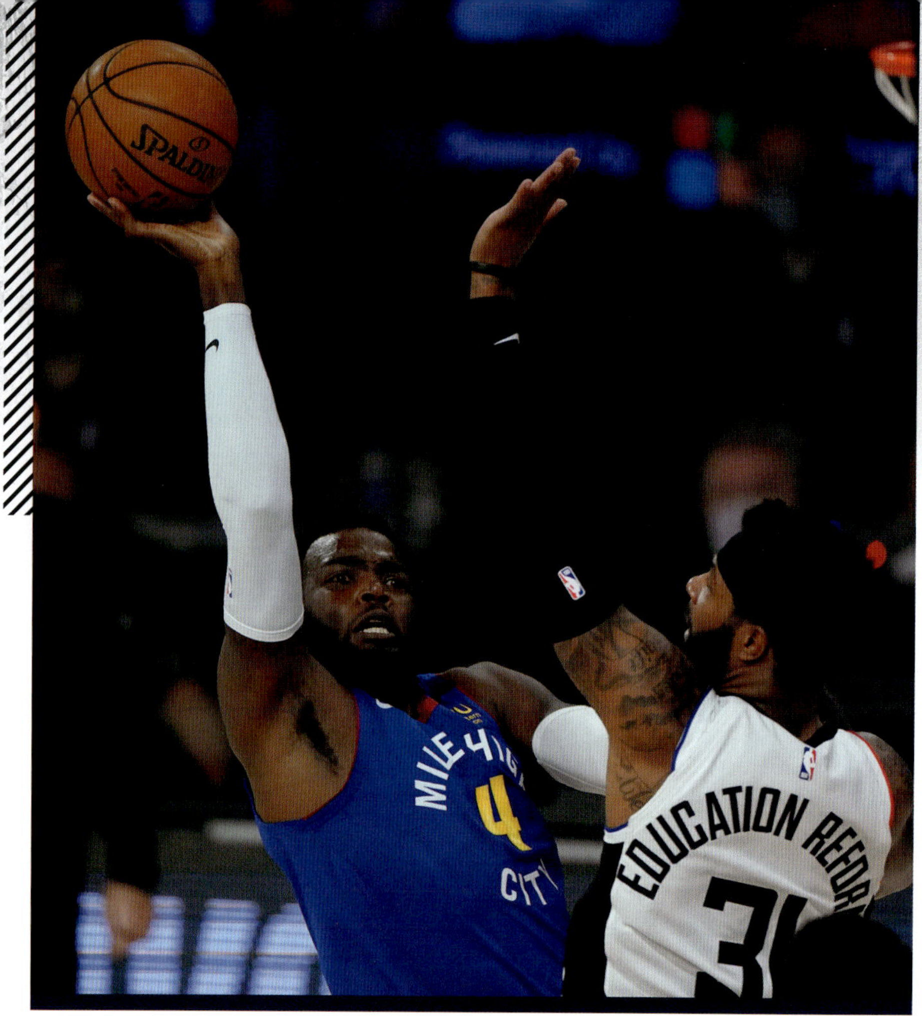

Paul Millsap shoots over a Clippers defender in Game 5.

FALLING BEHIND AGAIN

The Nuggets faced another tough test against the Clippers. Forwards Kawhi Leonard and Paul George had carried Los Angeles to its 3–1 edge. Two of the wins had come by double-digit margins. Los Angeles was one of two teams in the Western Conference with a better record than Denver in 2020. Now the favored Clippers were ready to finish the job.

The Nuggets didn't exactly come out swinging in Game 5. Denver trailed by 16 points as halftime neared. George and Leonard combined for 27 points on 10-for-16 shooting. Things looked bleak for Denver. That's when veteran forward Paul Millsap decided it was time to fight back, in more ways than one.

Millsap was frustrated with getting pushed around by the Clippers. As the clock wound down in the second quarter, he got into an argument with Los Angeles forward Marcus Morris. Teammates had to separate the players. Morris received a technical foul for unsportsmanlike behavior. The Nuggets were awarded a free throw.

Millsap's actions did more than give Denver a much-needed point. They also fired up the rest of the team. It helped that Millsap made sure his play matched his emotions. He erupted for 14 points in the third quarter.

Millsap's inspired play helped Denver get back in the game. Los Angeles's lead was down to seven points when the fourth quarter began. Before long, Millsap's teammates joined him in the fight. Jokić hit a three-pointer with just over seven minutes to go in the game. The shot put Denver in front for the first time, 89–88.

The game stayed close. With 1:15 to go, the Nuggets led 102–100. Jokić held the ball at the top of the key before rifling a pass to forward Michael Porter Jr. on the right wing.

Michael Porter Jr. reacts to his three-point shot that put the Nuggets up by five late in Game 5.

The 6-foot-10-inch Porter was being guarded by a much smaller player. He shot over the defender and drilled a three-pointer. It was his only shot of the game, but it was a big one.

The final score was 111–105 in Denver's favor. Nuggets head coach Mike Malone credited Millsap's decision to mix it up with Morris as the turning point in the game. "He stood up. His response to the situation helped our team respond," Malone said. "That gave us a group toughness."

COMEBACK, PART TWO

George and the Clippers told reporters after the game that the loss was no big deal. The Clippers still led the series 3–2. But the Nuggets shook that confidence again in Game 6. Once again George and Leonard helped the Clippers to a big lead. Their combined 31 points in the first half put Los Angeles up 63–47 at halftime. But the Nuggets controlled the second half. Led by Jokić, the Nuggets dominated the final 24 minutes. They pulled away for a 111–98 victory. Denver's star center put up 34 points, 14 rebounds, and seven assists in the win.

Game 7 happened to fall on coach Malone's birthday. Jokić joked that his coach would get one of two presents—a spot in the Western Conference finals or a trip home to his family.

In truth, Jokić had only one gift in mind for his coach. Once again the Nuggets had to deliver the hard way. They fell behind by 12 points in the second quarter and were down seven early in the third.

However, the rest of the game was all Denver. Jokić achieved a triple-double before the third quarter was over. He set a Nuggets playoff record with 22 rebounds. Murray handled most of the scoring. He finished the game with 40 points. And his 29-foot three-pointer with 8:48 left in the fourth put the Clippers away. The shot gave Denver an 89–74 lead. The Nuggets ran away with a 104–89 rout.

The team's historic comeback was complete. Denver moved on to the West finals. There, the Nuggets were finally eliminated in a five-game loss to the Los Angeles Lakers. Denver returned home after two magical months in Florida. A large crowd of family and friends greeted the Nuggets at the airport to celebrate the franchise's best season in more than a decade. They greeted a group that had elevated the once-struggling Nuggets to the status of true NBA contenders.

Jokić (15) and Denver head coach Michael Malone, *right*, celebrate the Nuggets' victory over the Clippers in Game 7.

CHAPTER TWO

MILE-HIGH HISTORY

The American Basketball Association (ABA) was founded in the mid-1960s as a rival to the NBA. Denver wasn't originally part of the league's plans for the opening 1967–68 season. The league had a franchise in Kansas City called the Larks. But owner James Trindle couldn't find an arena for the Larks in Kansas City. So before playing a single game, he moved the team to Denver instead.

Trindle didn't last much longer as the team's majority owner. Two months after the move, and still before the team played a game, he sold the Larks in June 1967 to William Ringsby. The new owner also had a company called Rocket Truck Lines. He ditched "Larks" as a nickname and called the team the Rockets.

It did not take long for the Rockets to take off in the "Mile-High City," as Denver is known. Many ABA franchises

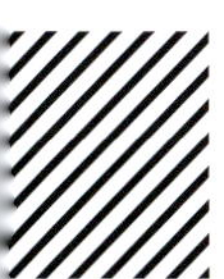

Before they were known as the Nuggets, Spencer Haywood was one of the Denver Rockets' first stars.

David Thompson, *left*, goes up for a dunk against the New York Nets in 1976.

struggled to survive. But the Rockets quickly became one of the new league's top teams. By their third season, in 1969–70, they were the ABA's Western Division champions. Their best player was one of the youngest in professional basketball. Twenty-year-old center Spencer Haywood was named the league's Rookie of the Year. He was also the ABA's MVP as he led the league in both scoring and rebounding. The next season, however, Haywood left Denver for the NBA.

For a few years, the Rockets sputtered. Before the 1974–75 season, Denver changed its nickname from Rockets to Nuggets. The move came in anticipation of a switch to the NBA, where the team in Houston was already called the Rockets. The new name also honored the people who mined the Rocky Mountains for gold and silver nuggets in the 1800s.

The newly renamed team struck gold on the court too. Head coach Larry Brown led the Nuggets to the best record in the ABA in each of the next two years. However, the team failed to win a championship. The Indiana Pacers upset Denver in the 1975 Divisional finals. The next year, star guard David Thompson led Denver to the ABA Finals. But in the final year of the league, the Nuggets lost to the New York Nets in the championship series.

SWITCHING LEAGUES

After that series, both the Nuggets and the Nets were moving on. The NBA and ABA merged, and four ABA teams switched leagues. Joining the Nuggets and Nets in making the move were the Pacers and the San Antonio Spurs.

The Nuggets and their high-powered offense had no problem adjusting to the NBA. Fans flocked to McNichols Sports Arena to watch Thompson's high-flying dunks. Denver claimed the Midwest Division title in its first NBA season. A year later, the Nuggets won their first playoff series and

Denver forward Alex English made the All-Star team every year from 1982 to 1989.

advanced to the Western Conference finals. There they lost in six games to the Seattle SuperSonics.

Denver's early NBA teams featured some of the most gifted scorers in basketball. Along with Thompson, the Nuggets trotted out high scorers like forwards Alex English and Kiki VanDeWeghe, as well as center Dan Issel. The Nuggets offense went to another level in 1981 when Doug Moe was hired as head coach.

Moe's philosophy on basketball was to let the shots fly early and often. Over the next ten seasons, with Moe leading the way, the Nuggets were one of the NBA's most entertaining and high-scoring teams. They also made regular playoff appearances.

Advancing in the postseason was tougher. The Nuggets reached the conference finals only once in that stretch. In 1984–85 the team finished 52–30. But the Nuggets could not get past the powerhouse Los Angeles Lakers. Denver lost the West finals 4–1.

ROCKY MOUNTAIN LOW

Moe left the team after the 1989–90 season. Denver immediately declined. The team spent the next 13 years suffering mostly losing seasons.

The Nuggets made the playoffs only twice in that time. But one of their postseason runs was memorable. In 1993–94 Denver finished 42–40. That was good enough for the eighth seed in the West. It also meant a matchup with the heavily favored SuperSonics, who had a record of 63–19.

Led by young center Dikembe Mutombo's shot-blocking, Denver pulled a shocking upset. After losing the first two games in a five-game series, Denver rallied to win three straight. It was the first time an eighth-seeded team had ever knocked off a number one seed in the NBA playoffs.

Denver nearly beat the powerful Utah Jazz in the

Go West? Maybe Not.

The Nuggets hired Paul Westhead to replace Moe as head coach in 1990. Like Moe, Westhead wanted his players to score quickly. Unlike Moe, Westhead's teams completely forgot to play defense. During Westhead's first season, Denver led the NBA in scoring at 119.9 points per game. But the problem for the Nuggets was that they also allowed 130.8 points per game, the most in league history.

An emotional Dikembe Mutombo leaves the court with the game ball after the Nuggets upset the Seattle SuperSonics in the 1994 playoffs.

next round. The Nuggets rallied from 3–0 down to tie the series before falling in Game 7.

After that playoff run, the Nuggets declined quickly. They hit a new low in 1997–98, finishing 11–71. The next season was shortened to 50 games due to an owners' lockout. Denver finished 14–36.

CONTENDING AGAIN

After another miserable season in 2002–03, Denver held the third pick in the NBA Draft. That year's class was loaded. The top prize was forward LeBron James. But three more players picked in the top five went on to all-time great careers.

Denver got one of them. Forward Carmelo Anthony had just led Syracuse University to the collegiate national title. The Nuggets snapped him up.

The team's fortunes improved immediately. Anthony helped Denver improve by 26 wins the next season and get back to the playoffs. The following season, Denver scuffled to a 17–25 start.

Carmelo Anthony attacks the basket against the Indiana Pacers in 2005.

George Karl was brought in as the new head coach. He led the Nuggets to a 32–8 finish and another playoff berth.

Karl and Anthony did not get along. But they won games together. In 2008–09 the Nuggets had their best record in two decades at 54–28. The team had made the playoffs five straight seasons but had yet to get out of the first round. That changed as Denver routed the New Orleans Hornets and Dallas Mavericks in back-to-back five-game series.

The Western Conference finals pitted Denver against the Lakers. Los Angeles downed the Nuggets 4–2. The long wait for an NBA Finals appearance continued for Denver fans.

The next trip would have to come without Anthony. He and Karl could no longer work together. Anthony thought his coach criticized him too much. Karl thought Anthony didn't pass enough or play strong defense. The superstar forward was traded to the New York Knicks in 2011.

The Nuggets thrived without him. Karl led the Nuggets to a 57–25 record in 2012–13. He was named Coach of the Year. But Denver lost in the first round 4–2 to the Golden State Warriors. It was the ninth time in a 10-year playoff streak that the Nuggets had lost their opening series. Despite the award, Karl was fired.

JOKER TIME

Denver was ready for a new era. But it took a few seasons to build. The Nuggets didn't make the playoffs again until the 2018–19 season. By that time, the team had a new superstar. And the Nuggets had found him in an unlikely place.

Most of the best NBA players are taken in the first few picks of the draft. Rarely do teams find stars in the second round. But when Denver selected Nikola Jokić with the forty-first pick in 2014, the team was getting a steal.

Jokić was playing professionally in his native country, Serbia. He didn't come over to the NBA for another season. When he did, he made an immediate impact. A threat for

Nikola Jokić, *right*, averaged more than 20 points per game for the first time in 2018–19, while also averaging 10.8 rebounds and 7.3 assists per game.

a triple-double every night, Jokić led the Nuggets back to winning ways.

He had help. Shooting guard Jamal Murray joined the team in 2016–17 as another scorer. Under head coach Mike Malone, Denver rose to new heights. The team won a playoff round for the first time in 10 years after the 2018–19 season. The next year, the Nuggets reached the Western Conference finals. They followed that up with another first-round win in 2020–21. It was the first time since joining the NBA that Denver had won a playoff series in three consecutive years.

Denver was experiencing a lot of firsts. Jokić became the first Nugget ever to win NBA MVP when he took home the award in 2021. The team had one of the league's top players, plus a solid supporting cast. It seemed like only a matter of time before the Nuggets would reach their first NBA Finals.

CHAPTER THREE

GOLDEN NUGGETS

Few players electrified basketball fans in the 1970s like David Thompson. The 6-foot-4-inch guard changed the way people thought about dunking. His 44-inch (1.1-m) vertical leap allowed him to fly at the rim. Thompson's aerial exploits earned him the nickname "Skywalker." But Thompson could do more than dunk. He was an excellent all-around scorer. Thompson won the ABA's Rookie of the Year in 1976 after averaging 26.0 points per game.

He then jumped to the NBA with the team and made three straight All-Star appearances as one of the best scorers in that league. In the last game of the 1977–78 season, Thompson racked up 73 points, the third-highest scoring game in NBA history at the time. Fellow NBA legend Bill Walton once said that Thompson was "Michael Jordan, Kobe Bryant, Tracy McGrady, and LeBron James all rolled into one."

David Thompson's spectacular dunks were a highlight for early Nuggets fans.

Thompson's teammate, center Dan Issel, had a less flashy nickname. He was called "the Horse" because of his durability. There were also times where it seemed the 6-foot-9-inch center never missed a shot. Issel relied on great footwork and a reliable jumper to average 20.7 points in 10 seasons with Denver from 1975–76 to 1984–85. Issel remained with the organization after retiring. He was the head coach when the Nuggets pulled off their stunning upset against Seattle in the 1994 playoffs.

BORN TO RUN

When Denver hired Doug Moe to be the head coach in 1980, the team was turning up the speed. Most coaches focused on defense and came up with various set plays to try to score. Moe, on the other hand, let his players make it up as they went along. The faster the Nuggets played, the better.

Moe's goal was to dare opponents to keep up. His critics often said his teams didn't play

Forward Kiki VanDeWeghe (55) joined the Nuggets late in 1980 after forcing a trade away from the Dallas Mavericks, who had drafted him the previous summer.

defense. Moe didn't care. He kept right on running to more than 400 wins in Denver.

It helped that Moe had the players to make his system work. Small forward Alex English led the NBA in scoring during the 1982–83 season. In fact, "the Blade" led all NBA players in scoring during the 1980s.

English played with a graceful style. He could knock down open jump shots or drive the lane. He was excellent at getting to the basket and drawing fouls. In 1988–89 he became the first NBA player to reach 2,000 points in each of eight consecutive seasons.

It took several players to make Moe's high-powered offense work. But Denver had a depth of talent. Forward Kiki VanDeWeghe made a pair of All-Star teams with Denver before he was traded to the Portland Trail Blazers in 1984. Guard Lafayette Lever, better known as "Fat," came to Denver in the trade. The nickname came from childhood, as his brother could not say "Lafayette." The nickname didn't quite fit the slim 6-foot-3-inch, 170-pound point guard. Lever was a reliable scorer, but he was at his best on defense. When he left the team in 1990, his 1,167 steals were a team record.

MOUNT MUTOMBO

By 1994 the Nuggets were no longer a fast-paced offense. Under new coach Issel, the Nuggets were a top-10 defensive team that season. That effort was led by one of the most unlikely NBA stars of all time.

Dikembe Mutombo was born in the Democratic Republic of the Congo. The central African nation is not known for producing basketball icons. Mutombo came to the United States to attend basketball power Georgetown University in the late 1980s. But he was not on the team. He wanted instead to be a doctor. Hoyas head coach John Thompson saw his 7-foot-2-inch size and added him to the roster. Mutombo soon became a star. In 1991 the Nuggets made him the NBA Draft's fourth pick.

Mutombo made a living swatting opponents' shots. He often added his signature move after a big block. The imposing center would stare his opponent down and wag his index finger in the player's face. Despite that taunt, Mutombo was one of the most generous NBA players ever. His humanitarian work focused mostly on improving living conditions in his home country. His service efforts earned him many awards during and after his career.

Dikembe Mutombo (55) was one of the most feared shot blockers in the NBA during the 1990s.

MELO TIME

The Nuggets entered the 2003 NBA Draft lottery hoping they could claim the top pick. The prize that year was high school

Carmelo Anthony, *left*, was a member of the talented 2003 NBA Draft class alongside LeBron James, *right*.

phenom LeBron James. Denver ended up with the third selection instead. Small forward Carmelo Anthony proved to be a great consolation prize. "Melo" turned the Nuggets around right away.

In his first season, the Nuggets improved from 17 wins to 43. That put the team back in the playoffs for the first time in nine years. By the 2008–09 season, the Nuggets were ready to make a run at the Finals. Melo's scoring was complemented by the leadership of point guard Chauncey Billups. Inside, Brazilian center Nenê provided toughness and rebounding. Forward Kenyon Martin and guard J. R. Smith were both extremely athletic. They flew around the court making plays. The group won two playoff series before falling to the Los Angeles Lakers in a tough six-game West finals.

Anthony was one of the NBA's most consistent scorers during the early 2000s. At 6 feet, 7 inches and 230 pounds, he was a matchup nightmare for opposing coaches. His soft touch from the outside allowed him to shoot over smaller defenders. But his driving ability allowed Anthony to get to the basket at will.

Anthony never backed down in big moments. "Captain Clutch" delivered again and again for Denver. During his time with the Nuggets, he made 14 game-winning shots.

NEW ERA NUGGETS

While Anthony was a sure prize in the 2003 draft, a decade later the Nuggets mined the second round for gold. They found it in yet another player from overseas.

Nikola Jokić didn't stay up to see whether he would get drafted. He was asleep in his home country of Serbia when the Nuggets grabbed him with the forty-first pick. Jokić was not tipped for stardom. Few teams knew about him when he joined the league a year later. The 6-foot-11-inch center is not explosive. He doesn't hammer home dunks at the rim. Instead, Jokić beats opponents by outthinking them.

Despite his size, Jokić is basically a point guard trapped in the body of a center. He loves to direct Denver's offense. His idea of fun is firing pinpoint passes from the top of the key or knocking down three-pointers.

It didn't take long before "the Joker" was Denver's key player. His vision, soft three-point touch, and excellent rebounding made him one of the game's best all-around threats. And soon he was making NBA history. Jokić's status as one of the league's best was cemented when he won the 2021 NBA MVP Award. He was the lowest draft pick ever to win it. A year later, Jokić became the first NBA player to ever record 2,000 points, 1,000 rebounds, and 500 assists in the same season.

Jokić received the perfect counterpart when sharpshooter Jamal Murray was drafted in 2016. The former University of Kentucky star quickly became a top offensive threat. He showed those skills during the team's 2020 comeback against the Utah Jazz in the opening round of the playoffs. Needing

Nikola Jokić was the first Denver player to win an MVP award since Spencer Haywood was named ABA MVP for the Denver Rockets in 1970.

to win Game 6 to stay alive, Murray poured in a career-high 50 points as the Nuggets won 119–107.

Murray was sidelined by a knee injury in April 2021 that forced him to miss all of the 2021–22 season. Denver fans eagerly awaited his return. Partnered with Jokić, Denver was poised to rise to Rocky Mountain heights.

CHAPTER FOUR

ROCKY MOUNTAIN MOMENTS

As the ABA drew to a close in 1976, the Nuggets were in contention for the league's last title. But they faced a stiff challenge from the Kentucky Colonels in the semifinals. The series went to seven games. Denver led Kentucky by a single point at halftime of Game 7. But rookie forward David Thompson turned it on in the second half.

When the game was over, Thompson had shot 13-for-20 from the field. He also hit 14 of 16 free throws. His 40 points and 10 rebounds paced a 133–110 win. Though the Nuggets fell in the championship series to the New York Nets, they left the ABA with fond memories.

THE BEST OFFENSE IS A GOOD DEFENSE

The Nuggets of the 1980s were known for their high-flying offense. That was certainly true in 1984–85. The Nuggets,

David Thompson averaged 26.4 points per game during the Nuggets' run to the 1976 ABA Finals.

Alex English (2) takes a shot against the Los Angeles Lakers.

headed by All-Star forwards Alex English and Calvin Natt, finished 52–30. The team led the NBA by averaging 120.0 points per game. And they gave up more than 117 points.

Offense ruled the first four games of the team's opening-round playoff series with the San Antonio Spurs. But in the deciding Game 5, Denver clamped down. The Nuggets forced the Spurs into 24 turnovers. They also held San Antonio to 39.2 percent shooting. Denver rolled to a 20-point halftime lead and never looked back. The final score was 126–99. It was the first time either team had scored less than 100 points in any series game. Denver had held only four opponents under 100 points all season.

That trend didn't last through the next two rounds of the playoffs. Denver allowed an average of 125.1 points to the Utah Jazz and Los Angeles Lakers. The Nuggets lost to Los Angeles in five games during the West finals. In Game 5, the Lakers won 153–109.

THE UPSET

Denver's playoff team in 1994 wasn't expected to do much. The Nuggets finished just 42–40 that year to claim the West's eighth seed. The young team didn't have much playoff experience. And they were facing the top-seeded Seattle SuperSonics. The 63–19 Sonics boasted superstars in guard Gary Payton and forward Shawn Kemp.

An eighth seed had never beaten a first seed in the playoffs. So when Seattle took the first two games easily, fans around the league didn't take much notice. But the Nuggets held Payton and Kemp to just 17 combined points in Game 3. Denver won 110–93. Denver center Dikembe Mutombo blocked six shots in the win. Then he blocked eight more in a 94–85 victory in Game 4. Suddenly the Nuggets were on the verge of an amazing upset.

Denver still had to go back to Seattle to win Game 5. Once again Mutombo controlled the game defensively. He added eight more blocked shots. But Denver's normal offensive stars,

Near Miss

After upsetting the SuperSonics, Denver nearly pulled off another miracle in the second round against Utah. The Jazz took a 3–0 lead in the best-of-seven series. The Nuggets responded by winning three straight games, two of them by three points or fewer. Denver's dream run ended in Game 7, when the Jazz cruised to a 10-point victory.

Dikembe Mutombo, *right*, makes a move against the Seattle SuperSonics in the opening round of the 1994 playoffs.

forward LaPhonso Ellis and guard Mahmoud Abdul-Rauf, were struggling.

Denver's bench stepped up in the second half. Forward Brian Williams had 17 points and a game-high 19 rebounds. Backup point guard Robert Pack scored 19 of his 23 points after halftime. He helped Denver erase a nine-point deficit in the third quarter.

The game went to overtime at Seattle's Key Arena. The Nuggets fell behind three times in the extra session, but Ellis converted a three-point play with 1:26 left to put Denver up 96–94. Pack then added two free throws in the final minute for a four-point lead.

On its final possession, Seattle attempted several shots that missed the mark. With one second left, Mutombo secured a final rebound. As the horn sounded, he fell on his back while holding the ball above his head. A TV camera hovered above him and captured his face, screaming with joy. The image was one of the most famous NBA pictures during the 1990s.

ANTHONY BEATS THE BUZZER

It would be 15 years before Denver enjoyed more success in the playoffs. Carmelo Anthony was a full-fledged superstar by the 2008–09 season. The Nuggets won the Northwest Division and faced the New Orleans Hornets in the first round of the postseason. In Game 4, Denver left no doubt it was ready to be a legitimate contender. The Nuggets wiped out the Hornets in a 121–63 win. The 58-point margin of victory marked the biggest blowout in playoff history. Denver held New Orleans to 15 points or fewer in three of the four quarters. The Nuggets forced the Hornets into an incredible 26 turnovers.

Game 3 of the second round against the Dallas Mavericks was a lot tighter. The Nuggets trailed by four with 31 seconds left. Then Anthony took over. He slammed home a dunk to bring Denver within two. The Nuggets got the ball back with 6.7 seconds left. Denver set up a play for Anthony. After catching the inbounds pass, he dribbled to the right wing. Dallas defender Antoine Wright tried to foul him so Anthony could not attempt a game-winning three. The refs didn't blow

Carmelo Anthony celebrates his game-winning three-pointer against the Dallas Mavericks during the 2009 playoffs.

the whistle. The Mavericks sat stunned as Anthony hoisted a perfect shot. Later, he called it the biggest shot of his career at the time.

MURRAY MAGIC

The Nuggets were used to being underdogs throughout their history. But in 2018–19 the team finished 54–28. Only the Golden State Warriors had a better record in the West.

However, the Nuggets faced a struggle in the first round of the playoffs. The Spurs won two of the first three games, and Denver was in trouble. But then the Nuggets' two young stars stepped up. Nikola Jokić came close to a triple-double in Game 4 as Denver won 117–103. He nearly did it again in another Denver win in Game 5. Two days later, San Antonio rallied to force Game 7.

In front of a noisy crowd at Denver's Pepsi Center, the teams went down to the wire. Jokić and Murray once again stole the show. Jokić did get his triple-double, with 21 points,

Jamal Murray, *center*, splits two defenders for a dunk in Game 4 of the Nuggets' 2019 playoff series against the San Antonio Spurs.

15 rebounds, and 10 assists. The final assist came on Murray's jumper with 36 seconds left that put the Nuggets up 90–86.

After San Antonio didn't score on its next possession, Spurs coach Gregg Popovich screamed at his players to foul and extend the game. But the crowd was too loud. None of the Spurs could hear him. Denver dribbled out the clock and advanced to the second round. Denver's run ended there, but just a year later the Nuggets reached the Western Conference finals. Behind its two young stars, fans expected many more deep playoff runs to follow.

TIMELINE

1967

The Denver Rockets are one of 11 teams to join the newly formed American Basketball Association.

1970

Led by ABA MVP Spencer Haywood, Denver wins its first division title.

1974

To avoid confusion with the NBA's Houston Rockets, Denver changes its name to the Nuggets.

1976

In the Final ABA season, Denver reaches the finals but loses to the New York Nets. Denver then joins the NBA in time for the 1976–77 season.

1978

David Thompson scores a team-record 73 points in a 139–137 loss to the Detroit Pistons on April 9.

1981

Doug Moe is hired with 51 games left in the 1980–81 season. He coaches the Nuggets to playoff appearances in nine consecutive years starting in 1981–82.

1985

Led by forward Alex English, the Nuggets reach the Western Conference finals for the second time before losing to the Los Angeles Lakers in five games.

1994

Denver becomes the first number eight seed to knock off the top seed in the playoffs with a 98–94 win over the Seattle SuperSonics in Game 5 of the teams' first-round series.

2003

The Nuggets select forward Carmelo Anthony out of Syracuse University with the third pick in the 2003 NBA draft.

2006

Anthony leads the Nuggets to their first division title since 1987–88.

2009

Denver reaches the Western Conference finals for just the third time since joining the NBA.

2011

After years of feuding with head coach George Karl, Anthony is traded to the New York Knicks along with point guard Chauncey Billups.

2014

The Nuggets select little-known Serbian center Nikola Jokić in the second round of the 2014 NBA Draft.

2016

Denver takes guard Jamal Murray from the University of Kentucky with the seventh pick of the draft.

2019

Murray and Jokić team up to lead the Nuggets past San Antonio in Game 7 of the first round of the playoffs, the first postseason series win for Denver in 10 years.

2020

The Nuggets return to the Western Conference finals for the first time since 2009.

2021

Jokić becomes the first player in Denver history to win the NBA's MVP Award. He is also the lowest NBA Draft pick ever to win the award.

FACTS

FRANCHISE HISTORY
Denver Rockets (ABA)
(1967–74)
Denver Nuggets (ABA)
(1974–76)
Denver Nuggets (NBA) (1976–)

KEY PLAYERS
Mahmoud Abdul-Rauf
(1990–96)
Carmelo Anthony (2003–11)
Alex English (1980–90)
Dan Issel (1975–85)
Nikola Jokić (2015–)
Fat Lever (1984–90)
Antonio McDyess (1995–97,
1998–2002)
Jamal Murray (2016–)
Dikembe Mutombo (1991–96)
David Thompson (1975–82)

KEY COACHES
George Karl (2005–13)
Mike Malone (2015–)
Doug Moe (1980–90)

HOME ARENAS
Denver Auditorium (1967–75)
McNichols Sports Arena
(1975–99)
Ball Arena (1999–)
Formerly known as:
Pepsi Center (1999–2020)

DUNKING IN DENVER

Denver hosted the first-ever Slam Dunk competition. The event was part of the ABA's All-Star weekend in 1976. Julius "Dr. J" Erving won by taking off from the free-throw line and slamming the ball home.

DUELING IN DENVER

On December 13, 1983, the Nuggets and Detroit Pistons played the highest-scoring game in NBA history. Detroit edged Denver 186–184 in triple overtime. Even more impressive, the teams shot only four combined three-pointers. Each team hit one shot from outside the arc.

NOTHING'S FREE

On February 19, 2021, Nuggets guard Jamal Murray scored 50 points in a 120–103 win over the Cleveland Cavaliers. He was the first NBA player ever to reach 50 points without hitting a single free throw. Murray was amazing from the field. He shot 21-for-25, including 8-for-10 from three-point range.

PIONEER

John McClendon made ABA history in 1969 when he became the league's first Black head coach. McClendon went 9–19 during a brief stint with the Rockets.

GLOSSARY

assist
A pass that leads directly to a basket.

berth
A spot in a competition or tournament earned through previous results.

contender
A team that has a good chance at winning a championship.

deficit
The amount by which a team is trailing in a game or a series.

draft
A system that allows teams to acquire new players coming into a league.

durability
The ability to withstand injury or fatigue.

humanitarian
Characterized by concern for improving the welfare of humanity.

lockout
A work stoppage during which team owners decide to shut down a league until an agreement can be reached.

merge
To join with another to create something new, such as a company, a team, or a league.

rebound
To catch the ball after a shot has been missed.

rival
An opponent with whom a player or team has a fierce and ongoing competition.

rookie
A professional athlete in his or her first year of competition.

steal
To take the ball from a player on the other team.

triple-double
Accumulating 10 or more of three certain statistics in a game.

BOOKS

Flynn, Brendan. *The NBA Encyclopedia for Kids*. Minneapolis, MN: Abdo Publishing, 2022.

Mahoney, Brian. *GOATs of Basketball*. Minneapolis, MN: Abdo Publishing, 2022.

Ybarra, Andres. *Great Basketball Debates*. Minneapolis, MN: Abdo Publishing, 2019.

ONLINE RESOURCES

To learn more about the Denver Nuggets, please visit **abdobooklinks.com** or scan this QR code. These links are routinely monitored and updated to provide the most current information available.

ABOUT THE AUTHOR

Will Graves has worked for more than two decades as a sports journalist. Since 2011 he has served as correspondent for the Associated Press in Pittsburgh, Pennsylvania, where he covers the National Hockey League, the National Football League, and Major League Baseball as well as various Olympic sports.